Tidying-Up

How to Clean Your House Fast & Easy

By

Odette Coralie

Tidying-UP

Copyright © 2017

ISBN: 9781520259635

Warning and Disclaimer

Publisher Contact

Skinny Bottle Publishing

books@skinnybottle.com

Why being tidy is necessity, not an option

Being tidy is a lifestyle and it is a choice. Being tidy can mean neatness in personal appearance and personal things, keeping a room, house or surroundings clean or having things in proper order.

There is this old saying that goes "Cleanliness is next to godliness". Sure some may say it is a load of bull but if you think about it, there is a lot of truth to that statement. Let me break it down for you. When you think about gods, deities and people in high places, do you imagine them doing the laundry or worrying about keeping the dwelling places spic and span? No. They seemingly have carefree lives with time for leisure and all the good things.

When you make being tidy a lifestyle, you will not have to worry about it so often and you will be able to live a life that is more meaningful, carefree, luxurious and more to your liking. More godly, if you will.

Now you may be thinking that living like that is not your thing so tidiness is optional, right? Wrong! Being tidy is a necessity that has ample benefits.

Being tidy saves time.

Studies show that you can sleep better, work better and generally function more in a space that looks, smells and feels clean. People tend to dilly-dally and procrastinate when their spaces are cluttered or dirty.

It is easier to find the things you need. No more rummaging through your closet for your favorite outfit, no more hearing "Mom, did you see my..." or turning your bag (or car) inside out just to find your keys.

No more mad dash to make your home, apartment or dorm room look presentable when you are having people over if it is always neat.

Being tidy saves money.

And because you can find things easily, you save money by not buying duplicates or triplicates of something you still have (which tends to happen when you can't find what you were looking for). Fewer chances of hoarding is always a good thing!

You are less likely to fall victim to pest infestation when you keep your place tidy. No need to pay for the exterminator!

Maintaining a clean home ensures that your investment in furniture and appliances are not wasted. They stay working well for a longer period of time, so you don't need to replace them often.

A tidy home is a better home.

You are more likely to utilize and enjoy your spaces if they are neat. That inner chef is hard to bring out if your kitchen is grimy and that artsy side of yours may stay unnourished in a workroom that is filled with clutter.

If your spaces are tidier, you can expect people in your home to also be a bit healthier. Airborne disease and respiratory infections are less likely to invade your home if it is kept well. Less dust and allergens for people with asthma, more opportunities for you to breathe easy too.

People in a cleaner, more organized home tend to have a better disposition. When there is space for everything (and everyone), people at home are not as irritable. For example, a tidier home makes getting ready for the morning a breeze, even on days when you wake up a little later than usual. You and your partner will not be bickering about the dirty dishes or missing socks if you both keep your home spic and span all the time.

Let's face it, a tidy home is a better-looking home. A small neat house beats grand places with junk in it, any day. Others admire a home that is neat and well put-together. Whether you like having guests over for dinner parties, barbecues or simple get-togethers, you will surely be the envy of others if your home is not embarrassing. Plus, a tidy house makes others think you have life figured out and you're one step ahead – who doesn't want that kind of good impression, right?

Keeping a home tidy is a team effort if you live with other people in a household. It can be a test of friendship and cooperation of the family. Children who grow up in a tidy home, with parents, teaching them to take part in chores develop discipline and several other values early on.

Why is tidying up such a chore?

There is no other way around it, most people think that tidying up is a chore. This is why many people rarely take their time to really tidy up and even more people never think of cleaning as a possibly enjoyable and rewarding task. So what makes tidying up such a despicable activity?

It is a dirty job.

After all, it is not called tidying up if you will be tackling pristine spaces. Whether it is the cupboard, the bottom drawer or your bag – tidying up means you have to work your way through a mess to turn it around. It is a reality of life that houses are not meant to be 100% clean and magazine-worthy all the time. It is bound to get messy here and there because people use the spaces.

In simple cases, tidying up can mean wiping the counter tops or dusting the windows; it gets much harder (and dirtier) when you haven't been cleaning for a while – gunk in your kitchen sink, expired food in your pantry or stinky socks under the bed. Tidying up is never glamorous, it never will be. But a tidy space is worth all the effort—I promise!

It takes time... A lot of time... And effort, too.

Tidying can be overwhelming. And anyone who has seen the show 'Clean House' or one of those home makeover shows knows that a messy house takes days and an entire team to turn around. But here's the thing – these shows depict extreme cases; not every home is packed with that much clutter or dirt.

Anyone who resolves to really tidy must allocate time and energy to do so. Depending on the amount of work to be done, tidying can be done in as little as 10 minutes (e.g. getting dirty clothes off the floor and putting them in a hamper, putting dishes in the washer and giving the counter a quick wipe-down) and as long as a full day or two (e.g. cleaning up and reorganizing an entire pantry or closet).

People have the tendency to fixate on the time and effort it takes to tidy up and in turn put off the cleaning for later. This fixation is what causes the dirt and clutter build up, then it becomes a vicious cycle. When you say you're too tired to put clothes directly to your hamper and this happens too often, soon you would not be able to see the floor. Sometimes, all it really takes is a few minutes a day to make a difference towards a cleaner home.

Tidying up entails combating smells too.

Dirt almost always comes with smells. Whether it is the mold and mildew on tiles, the garbage you badly need to take out, the litter boxes you have to refresh, the storage boxes in the attic you have not opened in years or the contents of your refrigerator, cleaning up almost always means you will encounter the smell of something unpleasant. What's worse, the chemicals in cleaning products often give off smells too.

But should these smells discourage you from starting the process of tidying? Of course not. If you do it right, you would not have to deal with the smell for long. And... there is also habituation—the nasty smell seems to mellow down because our sense of smell "gets used" to it after a few minutes. So suck it up, breathe through your mouth, stop complaining and get cleaning!

Tidying up also means dealing with sentimental value.

One of the biggest (and often unresolved) issues that untidy people have is that they like to hold on to things because of their sentimental value. Some people collect stuff, others hoard stuff. There are also those that hold on to things from people from the past, loved ones that have passed away or those who hesitate to let go of things they never use because it was given to them by a family member.

Tidying up becomes so difficult to do because of the attachment that people have with material possessions. Things get cluttered and take up valuable real estate in the home because of the fear that letting them go means throwing away an important memory or a person. It seems illogical to some but it is a reality for most that this is a very hard thing to deal with.

It is hard to figure out where to start.

"I do not know where to start!" This is a common statement of people when asked why they do not tidy up. No matter if you live in a one-bedroom condo or a massive mansion, not knowing where or how to begin is what gets most of us stuck not wanting to do anything related to cleaning.

Here's a quick tip: start in a space that you use on a daily basis. Something like your desk, bedroom or bathroom would be a good place to begin. The reason behind this is simple – tidying up a space that you see or use every day will make you feel better about the area. You will also make you motivated to make other places in the home look as great.

Remember, tidying up is only a chore at the beginning. When you make tidying up a part of your daily life, you will find that it is not so hard to do at all. Cheer up, there is probably no one in the world who absolutely loves cleaning—you are not alone!

Simple steps for tidying up

Any amount of time spent not cleaning is precious time that can be invested in something else. Since we already know that tidying up is not our favorite task in the world, wouldn't it be great if we could all keep cleaning simple?

There are two main kinds of tidying: the large-scale tidying and the daily tidying. We've been going on and on here about cleaning being time-consuming simply because it is the truth. But it is only time-consuming when we're talking about large-scale tidying like Spring cleaning (or any seasonal cleaning for that matter) or reorganizing a space. However, there are smaller cleaning tasks that can be done on a daily basis as a way of maintaining a livable space.

For large scale tidying:

Empty the space

Any professional cleaner or organizer would tell you that taking everything out is the first step to creating a tidy space. Emptying the area allows you to take stock of what the space looks like bare and how much you have been housing in it. It also gives you a chance to wipe it down, spot possible repair scenarios and evaluate how you can better utilize the space.

With just this first step, people are often surprised at how many things they have, and how much they have neglected certain things too. It is also a time for the "hey, I haven't seen that in forever", "I have been looking for this" or "I didn't know I had that in there" statements.

Purge and sort

To ensure a tidier area, only the necessities should be allowed back in the space that you emptied. So the essential second step is actually a two-fold process of purging and sorting. How you go about this greatly depends on the kind of space or room you are working on. But as a general rule, you should have 3 to 4 piles (or bins) for "keep", "toss", "donate" and "sell". Anything that is expired or broken should go to the "toss" pile. If it is going to cost you more to have something repaired than to buy a new one, that item also needs to go to the "toss" pile. Anything that you have not used in the last 6 months, does not fit you anymore or anything you do not see useful can go in either the "donate" or "sell" pile. This will allow others can benefit from what you don't need. Keep only the things that you like seeing or using – the things that make you happy.

Now, do not fall into the trap of handing down your clothes, shoes, bags and other items to your family members without asking them first. You might just be encouraging clutter into their homes. The better idea would be to hold a yard sale or sell your stuff online and earn a few bucks on your old stuff.

Take your time with this step and you will reap not only the perks of a cleaner home but a lighter feeling of having less sentimental clutter too.

Some experts suggest to purge and sort in by room, others by category. It is suggested that you begin with perishable and kitchen items (because they are no-brainers to purge and sort), then clothes (since they can be further sorted by functionality and seasons, and they can easily be replaced), then books, then documents and save sentimental items last. This way you get the feel of progressing from easy to difficult. Starting with your mementos first, could get you stuck because those photos, letters or gifts could stir feelings that will make you not want to throw anything away.

Organize the space

Perhaps the biggest mistake that people make when trying to organize their space is to automatically head to the store and buy organizing bins. Sure, getting those nice containers can be necessary but that should not be the go-to when organizing. Too often, people fall into the trap of getting the bins, stuffing things in them and admiring a cleaner looking space. This does not work.

After purging and sorting, you have to re-asses your space and your needs first. Ask yourself, "What and who is the space really for?" then follow it up with "How do I/we want it to look?" These are just some things that will help you figure out where things go.

For example, say you are tidying up a children's playroom. You have to consider the number of children who will be using the room, the accessibility of the toys and materials, the ease of clean-up, the kinds of labels, etc. Another example is cleaning up your pantry; you will have to group together the snacks, spices, grains and other things according to function whereas in a craft room you may want to organize by color or brand of tools.

For daily/maintenance tidying:

1. No one ever wants to think about allocating an entire day to cleaning. Small actions done today lead to less effort and time cleaning tomorrow (or the weekend). If you fold your laundry right after taking them out of the dryer, wiping down the stove top after cooking or put the remote back right where it belongs, you will not have to worry about it later on. Small habits make a world of difference.

2. Incorporating a simple cleaning routine in your schedule will cut down your big cleaning tasks. Something simple like clearing out the bathroom counter or running a load of dishes before bed will help you wake up feeling less irritable and burdened by the amount of cleaning that you need to do the next day. So schedule a bit of cleaning a day the same way you would schedule watching your favorite television show. Remember - things that get scheduled, get accomplished.

3. Keep a squeegee in the bathroom and quickly get rid of excess moisture on the counter, sinks or mirrors. It takes just a few minutes but will help you cut down on the cleaning you need to do because there will be fewer molds, hard water and soap stains and scum if you do this daily.

4. Keep a cleaning caddy loaded with your cleaning supplies. Having easy access to your supplies will make you want to keep tidy more often. Have at least one cleaning caddy per floor of your home or one tucked away in every room so you do not have to waste time when your forget things in different areas of the house.

5. Use a disposable wipe to wipe bathroom and kitchen counters before going to bed. This will prevent the build-up of dirt, dust and hair on your counters.

6. If you have a family, the bin system is a great idea to keep in your garage. Have a recycling bin, a return bin (for items you need to take back to the store or library books due) and a donate bin.

7. To keep your bedroom looking clean, make sure to allocate 15 minutes on these tasks daily:

   o Keep clothes off the floor.

   o Make your bed each time you wake up.

   o Each time you leave the room, take anything that doesn't belong there and return it.

   o Make sure your surfaces (like bedside tables or vanities) are clear of clutter.

Tips when tidying up the house

Practice the first in, first out rule when it comes to food items.

To avoid overstocking of food items and ending up with a pantry filled with expired food, make sure to follow the first in, first out rule. Consume earlier purchased items first before buying new ones. It might be helpful to color code meat containers or write a "cook by" or "eat by" labels on your refrigerator items too. Those dates on food cans can sometimes be too small to even bother with. Another tip could be keeping the front row of cupboards or shelves with items that are closest to their use by dates and the newer ones at the back.

Learn restraint when shopping.

It is hard to keep a house tidy if you keep on buying stuff you do not have space for. Even if you get to clean a space really well but you start shopping and stuffing your closet, pantry or cabinets again... it is not going to stay tidy for long. When you are out shopping, ask yourself the following questions:

- o • Do I really need this?

- o • Do I really want this?

- o • Where will I use this?

- o • Does this have a home in my house?

- o • Will this make me happy?

If you ask yourself these questions and you end up unsure, wait for at least a week and if you still want the item, you may get it.

Labels really help.

They may not always be the most glamorous thing in the world but labels sure help a household run more smoothly. Labels make it easier to find things and put them back, and make it less confusing when you are faced with so many options (e.g. which wire goes where?). They are especially useful in closets, kitchens, and home offices. These days, labels are no longer limited to plain sticker ones that you print yourself. Now you can also opt for label makers (printer companies make them), washi tapes and so on. Labels can be as creative as you are from chalkboards to colorful vinyl to stickers—the possibilities are endless!

Contain clutter.

Here's a reality check – magazine and television homes are styled and maintained by professionals. And they look that way because the spaces are hardly used. Your home will not stay clean or clutter-free 24/7. But you can always contain clutter so it will be a bit easier on the eyes. Here are two ways to do it:

• Have a junk drawer in your kitchen or office for knick knacks and items you will sort through on a different day. Just make sure you periodically clean out your junk drawer or this will not work.

- Invest in multipurpose furniture like ottomans or seating with containers underneath. If your kid's toys are on the floor and the guests are on the way, you can easily stuff the toys there and return later.

- Have airtight bins ready for seasonal items that you rotate inside the home. Bring out only the items you need for that season and keep the rest in storage so you do not run out of space.

Digitize what you can.

Do you really still need a physical copy of your ex-boyfriend's love letters even if the paper is getting tattered or yellow? Sentimental paper items, including cards, letters or photos (to name a few) can be scanned and saved in several ways so you preserve the memory and the item without keeping the clutter. Plus, you can easily go back to these things on your gadgets when you need them since they are electronically stored. Is not that better than your mementos gathering dust on your shelf or storage boxes?

Go paperless.

Paper can be a huge contribution to clutter around the house. If you can, sign up for paperless billing. You not only save on precious counter space, you also have less paper clutter to file and contain plus... you help save Mother Earth too!

It is so easy to sign up for paperless and it is easy to monitor your bills online too. Just make sure to keep your passwords and electronic information safe at all times.

Additionally, you may want to go for ebooks or audiobooks instead of physical, hard copies. You still get the information, the stories and the knowledge without the bulk or space in your library.

o

Psych yourself up for it.

So you've made a date for cleaning but you still have to drag yourself out of bed to do it? Prepare a plan and psych yourself up for it.

• Have your tidying tools on-hand. Refill your cleaning solutions, make sure your rags and cloths are clean and ready, etc.

• Map out which rooms or areas you will work on for that day. Do not attempt to clean up an entire house in one go... that's crazy and unrealistic.

• Clean systematically. If you're doing a room, pick a direction (clockwise or counter clockwise) then tackle the space that way so you do not miss a spot or transfer dirt from one place to another.

• Play music while you clean. Remember how music helps when you work out or go for a run? This is also like that. Music can help motivate you so you don't notice the time.

• Avoid the temptation of watching television or Netflix while cleaning. It can be too distracting and you will not finish.

• Set a timer so you push yourself to finish on time.

• Set a reward for yourself even before you start tidying.

Invest in good cleaning appliances and tools.

By investing, I mean looking at the quality first, then the price. You do not have to shell out too much for an arsenal of cleaning stuff. A reliable vacuum cleaner (with attachments), a sturdy mop, microfiber cloths, a few pieces of spray bottles (if you want to make DIY cleaning solutions), handheld vacuum, rubber gloves, squeegee, cleaning toothbrush and a loaded cleaning caddy would be the basics.

Once you get the most use of your cleaning tools, you can then explore (or upgrade) your arsenal to include organizing tools, essential oils, label makers and so on. But for the meantime, stick with the basics and you're good to go.

Aim for consistency, not perfection.

Tidying one time is not going to cut it. Having a clean home every day means you have to really stick to it on a daily basis. Which is why cleaning is really about finding a routine, finding products and techniques that work for you. Wanting things to be perfect is not going to help you, instead, it will just frustrate. Being consistent in your cleaning habit is what's going to make a difference towards a cleaner space. So when you find a cleaning schedule or hack that works for you, stick to it and watch the magic happen.

Clean primarily for yourself, not for others.

Each of us has pet peeves related to our home. For some it is the dirty dishes, others hate dragging mud into the halls while some absolutely abhor pungent odors. We are different and so are our characteristics. If you live with someone in the house who does not like to clean as much, just do your part and make sure they know their part. If you force others to clean, they're not going to do it and it will just stress you out.

Tidy up because you like the feeling of a clean space and you know the good things in store for you. That feeling of accomplishment right after a cleaning task should be enough for you, so try to not criticize others for what they do not do.

A quick tip, though, if you set goals, rules and cleaning routines together, you will probably have higher chances of getting others on board the cleaning boat with you.

Do not neglect the smells.

As we have discussed in previous sections, the scent of your home matters too. Even if your house looks spiffy, if it smells stuffy, you have work to do. Make sure that your house smells fresh and clean once you are done tidying up. You can do this by using scented candles, fabric/room sprays and reed diffusers, just to name a few.

Needless to say, taking the garbage out, keeping the exhaust on, cleaning dirty dishes and laundry on the daily also keeps smells at bay.

Try these cleaning hacks to save time, effort and money:

• Keep a bin or basket in your family room or any other common area for the items that easily get misplaced. It will save you time to return the items if they are all in one place instead of going back and forth to pick up items and return them. This is especially useful if you have several floors in the house.

- When dealing with spills, especially on your couch or carpet, try to pre-treat as soon as possible if you do not want to end up with stains. You can use a stain remover or DIY it with hydrogen peroxide and dish soap.

- Teach children to put things back where they belong starting with toy bins labeled with the name or pictures of the items. If you get them started early, you will not have problems asking them to be tidy later in life.

- Make it a habit to clean from top to bottom, left to right so you do not miss a spot.

- Line your garbage bags (especially those in the kitchen and bathroom) with a few layers of newspaper to help absorb liquids (that may leak) and odors.

- To clean up grease stains on clothing or furniture, blot off the grease with a paper towel then sprinkle with cornstarch or baby powder. The powder will absorb the oil and crust up. Launder or vacuum as usual.

- For greasy fingerprints or handprints on walls, draw on the prints with a piece of white chalk and let it sit for a few minutes. Wipe the chalk away with a damp cloth.

- Use a squeegee in short strokes to lift pet hair off your carpet.

- Annoyed by tops and blouses slipping off hangers? Slip the garment tag through the hook of the hanger. Alternatively, wrap pipe cleaners (or fuzzy wires) onto the hanger to keep clothes still. When clothes stay on the hangers there will be less cleaning up to do.

- To clean a blender quickly use, fill it halfway with lukewarm water and a pump of dish soap. Blend, rinse well and leave it to dry.

- Want to get clean clothes faster? Put a clean, dry towel in your dryer with the wet clothes. The dry towel will absorb moisture and make drying much faster.

- For a sweet-smelling bathroom, put a few drops of essential oil onto the tissue paper tube. The scent will be absorbed by your toilet paper and will radiate onto the bathroom.

- Keep the toilet bowl brush tidy and bacteria-free by letting it drip-dry in between the toilet seat and the toilet bowl. Do this before putting the brush back in the container.

- Keep small items from falling down the bottom of the dishwasher by using a delicates bag (the mesh bag used for laundry). This works well for measuring spoons, container lids, and even children's toys.

- Keep clothes and linens free from static cling by putting a 2 aluminum foil balls (about 2 feet worth, rolled into smooth tennis-sized balls) with your load of laundry.

- Invest in a good oven liner so you never have to clean the bottom of your oven again.

- To make it easier to get the gunk off your pots and pans, presoak them with warm water, dish soap, and baking soda. Allow to sit while you enjoy your meal and the icky stuff will come right off when it is time for you to wash them.

- When wiping down mirrors, refrigerator doors and anything vertical, do so in an S pattern instead of the buffing motion. Wiping from the top to the bottom will prevent the cleaning tool from picking up dirt from other spots and redistributing them.

- If possible, do not bring outdoor shoes into the house. They bring dirt, bacteria, and allergens. Use a tray for shoes near the door for you and your guests.

- Microfibre cloths are best for cleaning and dusting. They do the job well and do not leave streaks.

- Use a small paintbrush or old make-up brush on small or delicate items.

Stock up on some common supplies for DIY cleaning goodness.

Baking soda

- 50% baking soda, 50% water gets rid of scuff marks or crayon marks on the wall

- To clean a nasty-smelling drain, pour 1 cup baking soda on the drain and let it sit for about one hour. Pour 2 cups of boiled white vinegar then rinse with running water.

- Plain baking soda makes for an effective grout cleaner.

- Sprinkle baking soda onto your litter box when you change it to combat the smell.

- Similarly, sprinkling baking soda on your carpet 30 minutes before vacuuming deodorizes it.

- Clean your dishwasher by putting in one cup of baking soda into the bottom of the dishwasher overnight. In the morning, run an empty load and your dishwasher will be tidy and odor-free.

- Mix together 1 tablespoon of baking soda and 1 tablespoon of white sugar and leave it on your ant infested area to get rid of the little creatures. You can also use coffee to make the ants go away.

- Combine 1 teaspoon of dish soap, 1 drop of essential oil, baking soda and water to make a paste. Use this to scrub bathroom surfaces.

- To quickly clean the toilet bowl, sprinkle half a cup of baking soda and let it sit for 30 minutes. Scrub with the toilet brush and flush.

Rubbing alcohol

- Spray a small amount of rubbing alcohol on stainless steel or chrome surfaces (e.g. refrigerator door, cabinet handles) and wipe with a microfiber cloth. This will clear away fingerprints and dry streak-free.

- Make a disinfectant by combining 1 part rubbing alcohol and 1 part water in a spray bottle. Use this disinfectant spray to clean door knobs, light switches and other points of contact.

- Wipe away hairspray build-up on mirrors or sinks by using rubbing alcohol on a cotton pad.

- Refresh and disinfect cleaning cloths, sponges and mop heads by soaking them in rubbing alcohol.

- Spray rubbing alcohol on your keyboard and mouse to disinfect them.

- For cleaning screens (e.g. computer, television, tablet), combine 1 part rubbing alcohol with 1 part distilled water (it has to be distilled so that there are no minerals that could damage your electronics). Put on a cloth and wipe the screen. This solution dries instantly and gets rid of fingerprints too.

- For a countertop cleaner that is safe for all surfaces, combine 2 parts water, 1 part rubbing alcohol, 1 teaspoon dish soap and 10 drops of essential oil in a spray bottle.

Vinegar

• Make a window cleaner by combining 1 part water, 1 part white vinegar and a tablespoon of cornstarch in a spray bottle. Shake well and use on windows using a microfiber cloth and the S pattern.

• Combine 1 cup vinegar, 1 cup dish soap and water to make a solution that gets rid of soap scum in the bathroom. For tougher grease, let it sit for 5 minutes before washing away.

Dish soap

• For a cupboard cleaner, mix 1 part dish soap with 10 parts water in a spray bottle. Spray on the greasy cupboard surfaces, leave on for 5 minutes then wipe with a damp non-abrasive sponge.

• Bothered by unsightly weeds in the garden but do not like the smell of chemicals? Mix up two squirts of dish soap, ½ cup of salt and 1 cup of white vinegar in a spray bottle. Spray on weeds to get rid of them.

Borax

• Borax is a one-step toilet bowl cleaner. Sprinkle an ample amount of it into your toilet bowl before bed and when you flush in the morning, your bowl will be sparkling clean.

• To get rid of bugs, combine equal parts borax and white sugar. Place on a pest infested area.

• Mix a cup of borax with ¼ cup lemon to create a paste. Use it to erase sink stains. Rinse well and see your kitchen sink shine.

- Make a thick paste of borax and water. Apply onto molds and let it sit overnight. Wash in the morning and you will not even have to scrub – the molds will be gone!

Cornstarch

- In the absence of baking soda, cornstarch also helps clean up oil and grease stains. Simply sprinkle on the surface, leave it to crust before vacuuming or laundering the item.

- Blot up excess wood polish from your furniture by sprinkling some cornstarch on the surface. Let it sit for 10 minutes before wiping and buffing the wood.

Table salt

- To clean cast iron pans, fill the pan with water, sprinkle with ample salt and use a wooden spatula to scrape off grime. Alternatively, use dry table salt on a dry pan and use a gentle scrub tool to take off the debris. Wipe it dry and it will be as good as new.

- To deal with red wine spills, blot out the moisture using a paper towel then pour table salt on the wine stain. Let it dry overnight before vacuuming or laundering.

- To clean coffee or tea stains on stainless steel items, dump salt on the item then scrub with half a lemon. Rinse to wash away the stain.

- Clean a cutting board by pouring table salt and scrubbing the board with half a lemon (in a circular motion). This will get rid of the stains and smells while disinfecting the board too. Rinse and dry it well.

Lemon

• Make your fridge smell better with lemon. You can either leave a small bowl of freshly squeezed lemon juice or a fresh cut lemon in your refrigerator and the scent will be good for a week.

• Steam clean a microwave by putting a bowl of water with freshly squeezed lemon (include the fruit and the juice) and set the timer for 5 minutes on the highest setting. Let the microwave cool down for 5 minutes and wipe it down with a cloth or paper towel.

• De-scale your kettle by combining 1 part lemon juice and 2 parts water. Bring it to a boil, let it cool and rinse out the kettle.

• If you do not like the smell of vinegar but want a DIY glass cleaner, use 2 tablespoons lemon juice with 1 cup of water in a spray bottle.

• To rid your toilet bowl of the icky ring, squeeze half a lemon on the area and sprinkle with coarse salt. Use your toilet brush to scrub, flush and your throne will be clean.

• Clean away stubborn cheese stuck on your grater by grating the flesh of a lemon. The lemon oil and juices will loosen up the dairy. No more scrubbing and ruining your sponges!

• Make soap scum easier to wipe away from the shower or tub by using pure lemon juice on the surface. The acidity will counter the scum without being abrasive on the area.

• Rub half a lemon on chrome, copper or brass faucets, and fixtures to make them shiny again.

• Freshen up the garbage disposal by dropping the used lemon directly into the disposal and turning it on. The oils and acids will make the disposal clean and disinfected too.

Conclusion

Congratulations on taking the first step and plunging in, to achieving a tidy home. You have done a great job in picking up this book and reading it page by page!

Tidying up is one major stress in any household. It is right up there with the financial woes. The task of tidying up a home can bring forth so much bickering and arguing from figuring out who does what, for how long or how often should the task be done, and so on and so forth. A messy space can really cause anxiety, frustration, as well as stress. At worst, a messy space can even cause serious health issues and less productivity. However, as we have learned today, tidying up does not have to be all that stressful, nerve-wracking, or mind boggling and you do not need to be a rocket scientist to know how to tidy up.

With this book, you have been loaded up with useful tips, easy tricks on keeping a neater home. You can use this knowledge to keep any space, be it a home or an office, clean and tidy. If you have family members, you should share this book with them to get some work off your shoulders.

Being tidy is a good thing. It helps us practice discipline and organization not only in our homes but also within ourselves and our life in general. Hopefully, with the help of this book, you can start living a cleaner lifestyle for a much happier and organized you.

A tidy home is a treasure to cherish. The next time you feel like it is such a drag to clean your space, dump that idea and just think about all the awesome benefits that you will gain from having a neater house.

Remember that keeping a space tidy is not just a one-man show (unless of course you live alone); you should not be ashamed to ask your family members or your roommates to pitch in on the cleaning tasks – you all live in the same place after all. Everyone has to pull his or her own weight.

Always keep in mind that, it is the people who make the house a home. Therefore, when you make an efficient cleaning schedule work for you and your family, you also give yourselves the chance to live life fully – with more time for more important things such as bonding and having fun. So, what are you waiting for? It is time you get a pen and paper ready, jot down your cleaning schedule, meet up with the family and have them commit to some cleaning tasks. Sooner enough you will all be enjoying the fruits of your labor. Start tidying up and live a better life!

Win a free

kindle
OASIS

Let us know what you thought of this book to enter the sweepstake at:

http://booksfor.review/tidy

Printed in Great Britain
by Amazon